I'm Fine … I'm With the Angels

by Joyce A. Harvey
illustrated by Cliff L.Upp

To order additional copies of this book, contact:
Xlibris
844-714-8691
www.Xlibris.com
Orders@Xlibris.com

ISBN: Softcover   978-1-4134-0795-2
         Hardcover   978-1-4500-3555-2

Print information available on the last page

Rev. date: 04/20/2021

To my brave soldier Jennifer and all those who died while in service to their country.

J.A.H.

To my parents.

C.L.U.

ohnny didn't feel well. His head hurt and he was tired. It was Friday night and his favorite show was on television. He didn't care. He went to bed early.

Within minutes he was asleep. He dreamed of angels, but they didn't look like angels he had seen in pictures. They wore the type of clothes he wore and they didn't have any wings.

Johnny slept late the next morning. His mother was surprised when she didn't find him watching cartoons. She mentioned this to Johnny's father.

"Maybe he read too many comic books under the covers last night," he joked.

Johnny's mom peeked into Johnny's room and found him fast asleep.

Around 10:00 that morning Johnny got up and made his way to the breakfast table. He only nodded when his mother asked him if he wanted some cereal. His mind was on the angel dream he had. "Mom," he asked, "do you believe in angels?"

"Well, yes, I do. Why do you ask?"

"Oh, no special reason," Johnny said.

When Johnny wasn't feeling better on Monday, his mother called the doctor and made an appointment for the next day.

Johnny wasn't sure about this doctor stuff. "Will I have to get a shot?" he asked in a nervous voice.

"I don't know," his mother said. "I don't think so, but we'll see what the doctor says."

Johnny liked Dr. Jane. She always spoke directly to him and made sure he understood what she was saying. She wore a colorful smock decorated with animals. Seeing the animals always made him feel better. They reminded him of his favorite stuffed animal, an elephant he called "E-o." Johnny didn't take E-o out of the toy box very often. People might think he was too old to have a favorite stuffed animal, so he kept it hidden. He peeked at it often, but he didn't tell anyone. *Some things are best kept to yourself,* Johnny thought.

The next day, Johnny and his mother arrived at the doctor's office. Dr. Jane asked Johnny to stick out his tongue so she could see the back of his throat. Johnny thought it was funny he was allowed to stick his tongue out at his doctor, but not at his friends, or worse yet, at his teacher. He remembered the time he had to stand in the corner when his teacher turned around and saw him sticking his tongue out at her.

Dr. Jane felt the side of Johnny's neck. She said Johnny's glands seemed to be bigger than usual. She explained that glands have the job of cleaning bacteria out of the body. "Maybe they're working extra hard for some reason," she said.

Dr. Jane finished her exam and sat down to talk with Johnny and his mother. "Johnny," she said, "I want to test some of your blood. You will only feel a small prick and it will be over. Do you think you could let us do that?"

Oh no, Johnny thought to himself. *I knew there would be needles.* What was he supposed to say at this point? *Why do adults bother to ask a question there's only one answer to?* he wondered.

"I guess so," Johnny said in a half-hearted response. His father served in the army and he was always telling Johnny to be a brave soldier.

"Good," replied Dr. Jane. I'll send the nurse in to draw your blood. "By the way, is cherry still your favorite flavor?"

Johnny nodded without much enthusiasm.

The needle stick wasn't so bad, and soon Johnny was out the door with a cherry sucker in his mouth and two in his hand for his younger brother, David, who was five, and his four-year-old sister, Tracy.

The next day when Johnny came home from school he noticed his mother's eyes were red. She looked as if she had been crying. She hugged him longer than usual.

His mother and father were very quiet at dinner. They didn't eat much. His father helped with the dishes that evening, which he usually didn't do.

When they were finished, Johnny's mother said she and his father wanted to talk with him. They sat down in the family room. "Johnny," his mother began, "Dr. Jane called with the results of your blood tests. Your blood cells aren't quite right, and that is why you have been tired lately. Dr. Jane thinks it would be best if you went into the hospital for treatment."

Johnny sat there listening. "How long will I be there?" he asked.

"I'm not sure," his mother answered.

"Son," his father said, "you've always been a brave soldier when you needed to be. We need you to be a brave soldier now. Your mother and I will be with you as much as we can."

Johnny thought his dad's voice sounded strange, as if he were going to cry.

"When do I have to go to the hospital?" Johnny asked.

"Dr. Jane thinks it would be best if you went tomorrow," his mother said.

"Tomorrow?" Johnny asked. "Why so soon?"

"Well, son," his father said, "the sooner you go, the sooner you will be feeling better." Johnny nodded. That made sense to him.

They all went into Johnny's room and packed his bag. His mother gathered things like his toothbrush and comb. He chose his favorite pajamas and some comic books. When his parents weren't looking, he put his flashlight in the suitcase so he could read under the covers.

His parents tucked him in that night. After they left the room, he lay wondering what the hospital would be like. He thought maybe this was a good time to have E-o with him. Johnny got E-o out of the toy box and tucked him safely in his suitcase.

He crawled back into bed and drifted off to sleep. He dreamed of a lady all in white. Was she a nurse or an angel?

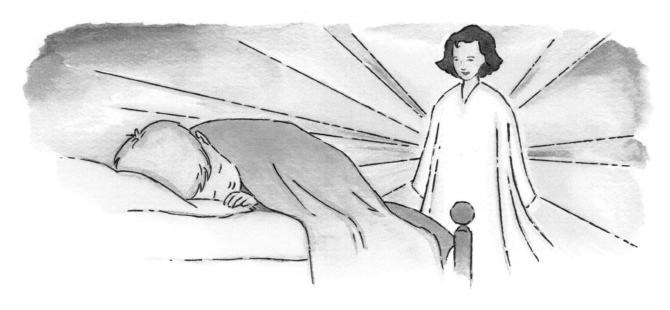

In the morning they drove to the hospital. Johnny was taken to the children's unit. He walked by a playroom and saw comic books and videos on the shelf. He thought he should check them out as soon as he had a chance.

A nurse named Bobbi helped him settle into his room. She was very nice and told him everything that was going to happen. She explained she would have to put a needle in his arm so medicine could flow into his blood. He didn't like hearing that. He looked at his dad for his response. His dad nodded and saluted. He thought he was going to get the "brave soldier" talk again, but his dad didn't say anything. Actually, his dad didn't look so brave just then. His face looked white and he sat on a near-by chair.

Bobbi was very quick with the needle and the medicine was flowing into Johnny's arm before he even realized it.

Several days went by, and Johnny was still in the hospital. He wondered just how sick he was. When he had chicken pox, his mom and dad didn't seem as nervous as they were now. He wondered if he were going to die. He had seen people die in the movies, even in cartoons. He decided to ask his mother.

"Mom, am I going to die?"

His mother looked upset by his question. "No, darling," she said. "You're going to be fine. It's just going to take some time." She left the room shortly after that and said she had to go to the bathroom.

As the days went by, Johnny began to ask his parents questions such as, "What is it like to die? Where do we go when we die?" He would also ask the nurses and Dr. Jane the same questions. Nobody seemed to want to talk with him about that. But he was curious. He wasn't feeling any better, even with all the medication.

One afternoon, a lady named Alice came into his room. She told Johnny his mom and dad said it was all right for her to see him. "I'm a social worker," she explained to Johnny, "which is just a fancy title for someone who likes to read books to kids. I understand you've been asking questions about Heaven and what happens when we die."

Johnny nodded.

"Would you like me to read to you a book about that?" Alice asked.

Johnny nodded again.

Alice reached into a cloth bag, took out a picture book and began reading to Johnny.

"When the body dies, a part of us continues to live. Some people call it the soul; others call it the spirit. Dying is like the process a caterpillar goes through as it spins a cocoon around itself. When it comes out of the cocoon, its form has changed to a butterfly. Before the caterpillar spins the cocoon it can only crawl. Once it comes out, it can fly.

"When we die, which some refer to as 'crossing over,' we shed our bodies like the caterpillar sheds the cocoon. Someone meets our soul or spirit and helps us to find our way into the light where God is. Some refer to this place as Heaven; others call it the 'other side.' The spirit who meets us may be a family member or a friend who has died before we do."

Alice asked Johnny if his grandparents were still alive. He said his Grandpa Hill died before he was born and he'd never met him. Alice told Johnny, "It doesn't matter if you don't know your grandpa, because Grandpa knows you. He will probably be there to greet you, no matter how old you are when you die. Even if Grandpa Hill doesn't meet you, there are spirits who help children make the crossing."

"Like the crossing guard at our school?" Johnny asked. "She watches the signal lights and walks with us across the street when it's safe."

"Yes, it is sort of like that," Alice answered.

Johnny asked lots of questions like: "Do pets go to Heaven?"

"Yes, they do," Alice explained. "In fact, there are spirits who take care of pets who die before their masters or family members cross over. Do you have a pet?" she asked Johnny.

"No, but I always wanted one," he replied sadly.

Alice and Johnny talked quite a while. She told Johnny, "As spirits, we can go anywhere we choose. We can visit our mom and dad whenever we want to. They may not always know we are there because they usually can't see us. Sometimes we can let them know by little signs we might give them."

Johnny felt better after their talk. Alice asked him if it would be all right if she came back again to visit. Johnny said, "Yes."

That night Johnny dreamed about angels again. He was sitting on a bench in a beautiful park. A young man with dark hair walked up to him. He looked like a teenager. He said his name was Mark and he wanted to meet Johnny. He had a cellular phone hooked on his belt and he was wearing sunglasses. Mark explained he was in spirit form. "I guess you could call me an angel," he said. "May I sit down with you?" he asked Johnny.

"Sure," Johnny said. He liked Mark already. He thought he was pretty cool. Any angel who carried a cell phone was okay with him.

"I understand you've been sick lately," Mark said. "I want to let you know when you come over to Heaven, I will be glad to greet you and show you around. Would you like that?"

"Sure," Johnny said. "Do you know when that will be?"

"No, I don't," said Mark. They were silent for a minute, and then Mark asked, "Do you want to meet some of my friends?"

Johnny nodded. Mark took Johnny's hand and they floated to another beautiful spot. Johnny had never floated before. He felt so light. He thought it was great fun, even more fun than the rides at the amusement park.

Johnny could see a girl coming toward them with lots of animals. She had dogs, cats, birds and even a horse with her. She had dark hair, brown eyes and was wearing a pager on the waist of her pants. She looked about the same age as Mark. When she got closer, Mark said, "This is my friend, Jennifer. Jen, this is Johnny."

"Hi Johnny," Jennifer said. "My job in Heaven is to watch over the animals that don't have homes yet. They either never had an owner, or their owners are still on the earth."

"Wow," Johnny said. "You're lucky. I always wanted a dog."

"Would you like to come with me and pick out a pet to have for your very own when you come to Heaven?" Jennifer asked.

"Could I really?" asked Johnny excitedly.

"Yes. Let's go. Do you want to ride on the horse with me?" Jen asked Johnny. He nodded and Jen lifted him up on the horse.

"See you later," Mark said as he reached to answer his ringing cellular phone.

Jen and Johnny rode to Jen's ranch. They got off the horse and walked over to the dog area. Johnny saw other spirits and angels helping with the animals as well. Jen introduced Johnny and explained he was there to pick out a pet.

Johnny chose a German Shepherd named Sarge. He thought "Sarge" was a funny name for a dog, but Jen assured him the dog's name really was Sarge. Jen was pleased Johnny picked Sarge, because he had belonged to her mother's family. Jen played with Sarge on earth before she crossed over to Heaven. Johnny thought his dad would be pleased as well. He used to talk about a man from the army he called "Sarge."

Jen told Johnny that on earth Sarge had medical problems too. "He was hit by a car and lost one of his legs," she explained. "But as you can see, here in Heaven everyone is whole and well again."

Johnny played with Sarge until Jen said it was time to go. They got on the horse and rode back to the park bench where Mark was waiting for them. Johnny got off the horse and waved good-bye to Jen.

"Sarge will be here waiting for you when you come. I'll take good care of him," Jen said.

Then Johnny woke up. He felt good about the dream and he remembered everything. He liked the idea of having his own pet and wondered if that would really happen.

When Alice came to see him that day, he told her the entire dream.

"It seemed so real," Johnny said.

"Maybe it was," Alice replied. "Sometimes people have what are called 'visitation dreams,' where spirits in Heaven visit us in our dreams."

"Do you think Mark is one of those crossing guards you talked about?" Johnny asked.

"It sounds like he might be," Alice answered.

"When I die, will I be able to visit Mommy and Daddy in their dreams?" Johnny asked. No one had told Johnny he was going to die, but he was beginning to think he might.

"Yes, you will be able to visit them," replied Alice. "It's one of the best ways to keep in touch with your family after you cross over. You can even hug them in their dreams and give them messages."

"Wow!" said Johnny. He never knew that.

He mentioned the dream to his mother. He also told her about his conversation with Alice. "Mom, do you believe that people from Heaven can visit in your dreams?" Johnny asked.

Johnny's mom thought for a moment. She looked as though she was remembering something. "I've had a couple of dreams about my father, your Grandpa Hill, after he died. I remember they felt so real. In one dream the only thing he said to me was, 'I want you to know I'm all right.' I always wondered about that dream. I felt like he was really there with me."

In the evening, when his father arrived, Johnny and his parents talked about dying and about visitation dreams. Johnny held tight to E-o the whole time they were talking. His mom and dad cried a little and so did he. But he was glad he could tell them about the dreams and talk with them about his questions. Even though his mother and father didn't tell him for sure he was dying, they did say it was a possibility. "We'll all die someday, Son," his father said.

    That night Johnny had another dream. This time an older man was standing
on a hill in the distance. He had light all around him. He waved at Johnny.

    When Johnny woke up, he thought about the man in the dream. He
looked like the picture of Grandpa Hill his mother kept on the fireplace
mantle. Johnny wondered if that's why the man was standing on a hill ... to
give him a hint that he was Grandpa Hill.

As the days went by, Johnny didn't seem to be getting any better. As a matter of fact, he was feeling worse. He decided it was time to bring up the subject again. He looked at his parents, who hardly left his bedside now, and asked them if he was dying. They looked at him and then at each other for a long time. Johnny's parents had always tried to be honest with him and they wanted to be honest now. They reached for his hands. His father took a deep breath and said, "Yes son, I think you are."

Johnny nodded. Somehow he already knew the answer. Johnny also knew it was hard for his dad to tell him the truth, just like it had been hard for Johnny to tell the truth when he had done something wrong. Johnny gave his dad a weak salute to let him know he was being a "brave soldier." His father saluted back and then began to cry. Johnny didn't want to leave his mother and father and David and Tracy. But it made him feel better to know he could still visit them.

That evening, there were a lot of people sitting around his hospital bed. He was very tired, and barely knew they were there. Suddenly, he saw a beautiful light up toward the ceiling. It was the brightest light he had ever seen. Then he saw them—Grandpa Hill, Mark, Jen and Sarge. They waved to Johnny and told him it was time for him to go to Heaven. He felt himself floating up from the bed. He looked down and saw his parents below him. They were crying.

He tried to tell them he was fine and that he felt better than he had in a long time. But he couldn't seem to get their attention. Mark explained to Johnny that his parents couldn't hear him right now, but later he would be able to let them know he was fine.

Johnny felt confused. He didn't want to leave his family, and yet he felt very peaceful. "I understand," Mark said softly, as if reading Johnny's thoughts. "At first, it was hard for me to leave my family. But you can come back in spirit form and visit them as often as you like. Right now though, we need to check you into Heaven. Once you get settled there, you can come back and visit."

Johnny began to pet Sarge, who was glad to see him. "Sarge is the perfect dog for such a brave soldier," Jennifer said.

Johnny turned to look back at his family. Tracy was looking directly at him with amazement. "She looks like she can see me," Johnny said.

Jen explained it is easier for little children to see angels and spirits than it is for adults. Tracy started to wave to him. Johnny waved back. Johnny's mother and father had their heads down on his bed and weren't looking in the same direction as Tracy. Johnny could see E-o lying on the bed. He hated to leave him behind, but Jen said Tracy and David would need E-o now to comfort them, just as he had always comforted Johnny.

"It's time to go now Johnny," Mark said. "You'll see them again real soon." Mark took Johnny's hand and they headed toward Heaven. Johnny didn't know quite what to expect in Heaven, but he felt safe with Grandpa Hill, Mark and Jen. He knew he could trust them as he trusted the crossing guard at school.

Johnny looked back at his family one more time. Tracy was still waving. Johnny shouted to her "Take good care of E-o for me. I'll come back soon and visit you in your dreams. And Tracy, please tell mom and dad I'm fine. I'm with the angels!"

To Be Continued... Johnny's Journey has just begun.

What will Johnny do when he gets to Heaven? Watch for the next book in the *I'm Fine ... I'm With the Angels* series: ***Johnny Angel***.

Printed in the United States
by Baker & Taylor Publisher Services